One of my favourite things about
being your uncle is having fun together.
Just imagine all the things we can do!

We can find critters on the beach
and in the forest too.

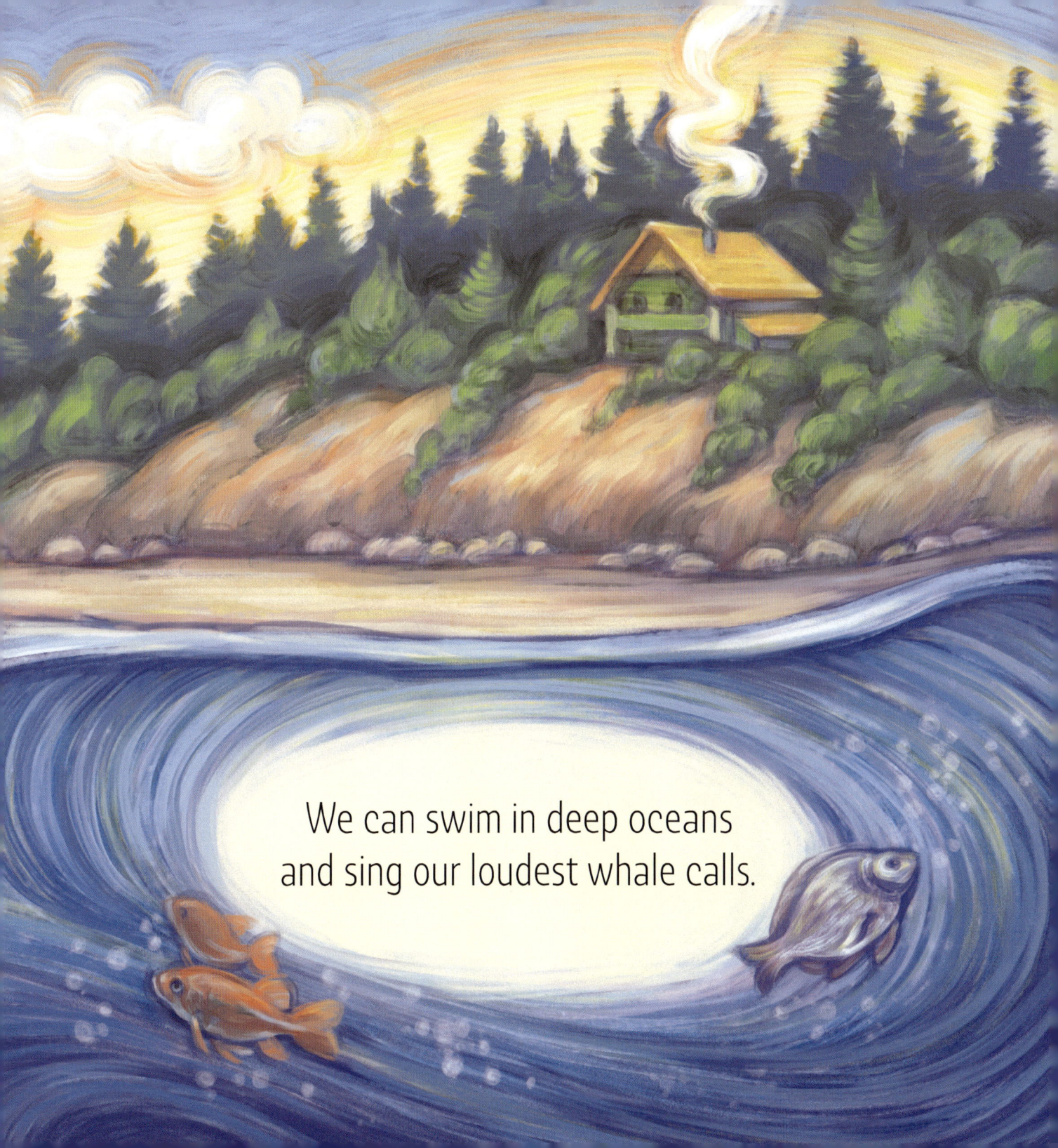

We can swim in deep oceans
and sing our loudest whale calls.

We can dance to songs
that make us smile and twirl
until we get dizzy.

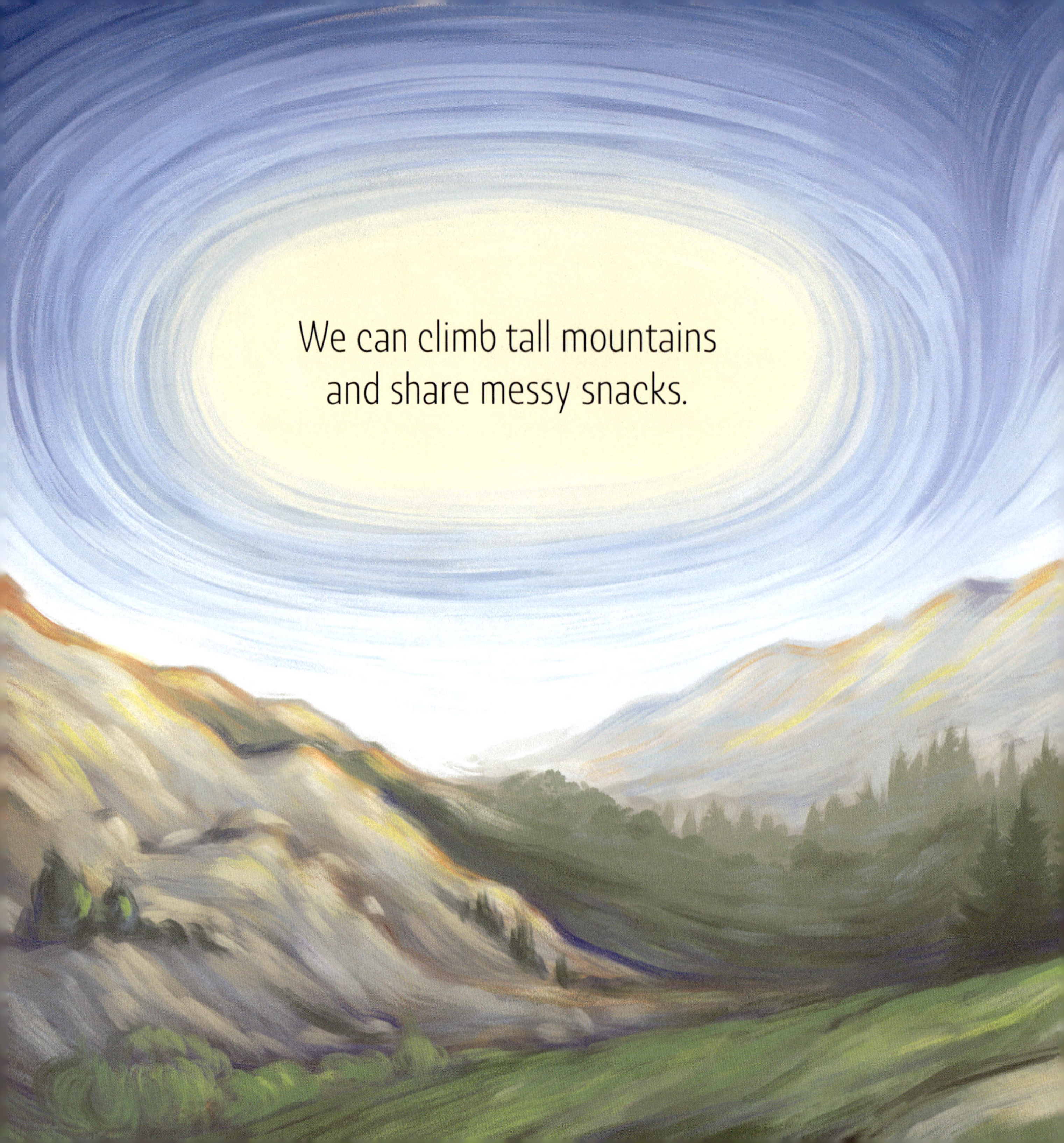

We can climb tall mountains
and share messy snacks.

We can learn how to play
new games and enjoy them
win or lose.

We can practice our painting skills
and mix and match bright colours.

We can act really silly
so the world can hear your belly laugh.

We can fix things if they break
and make them better than before.

We can fall on our faces and get up
to try again.

We can build big jumps
and fly off them for hours.

And at the end of the day, we can search for shapes in the stars and give them funny names.

Big or small, we can do it all.
I'm here when you need me.
I love being your uncle.

Printed in Great Britain
by Amazon